The Twelve Days of Christmas—in

TEXAS, That Is

The Twelve Days of Christmas—in Texas, That Is

By David Davis

Illustrated by Candace Camling

PELICAN PUBLISHING COMPANY
GRETNA 2011

For Win and Margaret Brisbin—DRD
For Mom and Dad. All my love—CC

Copyright © 2011
By David Davis

Illustrations copyright © 2011
By Candace Camling

The word "Pelican" and the depiction of a pelican are trademarks of Pelican Publishing Company, Inc., and are registered in the U.S. Patent and Trademark Office.

Library of Congress Cataloging-in-Publication Data

Davis, David, 1948 Oct. 29-
  The twelve days of Christmas—in Texas, that is / by David Davis ;
  illustrated by Candace Camling.
    p. cm.
  ISBN 978-1-58980-924-6 (hardcover : alk. paper) 1. Gifts—
  Juvenile poetry. 2. Christmas—Texas—Juvenile poetry. 3.
  Children's poetry, American. I. Camling, Candace, ill. II. Title.
  PS3554.A93344T84 2011
  811'.54—dc22

                          2011005200

Printed in Singapore
Published by Pelican Publishing Company, Inc.
1000 Burmaster Street, Gretna, Louisiana 70053

The Twelve Days of Christmas—in Texas, That Is

On the first day of Christmas my
darlin' gave to me . . .

A mockingbird in a gum tree.

On the second day of Christmas
my darlin' gave to me
Two silver spurs,
and a mockingbird in a
gum tree.

On the third day of Christmas my
   darlin' gave to me
Three oil wells,
   two silver spurs,
and a mockingbird in a gum tree.

On the fourth day of Christmas
my darlin' gave to me
Four javelinas,

three oil wells, two silver spurs,
and a mockingbird in a gum tree.

On the fifth day of Christmas my
    darlin' gave to me
Five armadillos,
four javelinas, three oil wells, two
    silver spurs,
and a mockingbird in a gum tree.

On the sixth day of Christmas
 my darlin' gave to me
Six flags of Texas,
five armadillos, four javelinas, three
 oil wells, two silver spurs,
and a mockingbird in *a*
 gum tree.

On the seventh day of Christmas
my darlin' gave to me
Seven jackrabbits jumping,
six flags of Texas, *five armadillos*,
four javelinas, three oil wells,
two silver spurs,
and a mockingbird in a
gum tree.

On the eighth day of Christmas my darlin' gave to me
Eight boots a'scootin',
seven jackrabbits jumping, six flags of Texas,
five armadillos, four javelinas, three oil wells,
two silver spurs,
and a mockingbird in a gum tree.

On the ninth day of Christmas
my darlin' gave to me
Nine bluebonnets blooming,
eight boots a'scootin', seven
jackrabbits jumping, six flags of
Texas, *five armadillos,* four javelinas,
three oil wells, two silver spurs,
and a mockingbird in a gum tree.

On the tenth day of Christmas
my darlin' gave to me
Ten tall Stetsons,

nine bluebonnets blooming,
eight boots a'scootin', seven
jackrabbits jumping, six flags
of Texas, *five armadillos*, four
javelinas, three oil wells, two
silver spurs,
and a mockingbird in a
gum tree.

On the eleventh day of Christmas my darlin' gave to me
Eleven broncos bucking,
ten tall Stetsons, nine bluebonnets blooming,
eight boots a'scootin', seven jackrabbits jumping, six flags of Texas,

five armadillos, four javelinas,
  three oil wells, two silver spurs,
and a mockingbird in a gum tree.

On the twelfth day of Christmas my
    darlin' gave to me
Twelve longhorns leaping,
eleven broncos bucking, ten tall Stetsons,
    nine bluebonnets blooming, eight boots
    a'scootin', seven jackrabbits jumping,

six flags of Texas, *five armadillos*,
four javelinas, three oil wells, two
silver spurs,
and a mockingbird in a gum tree.